PRACTICAL
HORSE WHISPERING

by
Perry Wood

Illustrations by
Carole Vincer

KENILWORTH PRESS

First published in the UK in 2003
by Kenilworth Press, an imprint of Quiller Publishing Ltd

Reprinted 2005, 2006, 2009, 2011, 2012, 2013

British Library Cataloguing-in-Publication Data
    A catalogue record for this book
    is available from the British Library

ISBN 978 1 872119 67 0

Printed in China

Kenilworth Press
An imprint of Quiller Publishing Ltd
Wykey House, Wykey, Shrewsbury, SY4 1JA
Tel: 01939 261616 Fax: 01939 261606
E-mail: info@quillerbooks.com
Website: www.kenilworthpress.com

CONTENTS

PRACTICAL
HORSE WHISPERING

4 What is horse whispering?
5 Equipment for horse whispering
6 Round pens and the alternatives
7 Understanding the horse's language
10 Human body postures for horse whispering
12 Hand, voice and breathing signals
13 Getting horses to follow you – method 1
17 Getting horses to follow you – method 2
19 Leadership, body space and boundaries
20 Taming the wild side
20 Running with horses
21 The magic touch – stroking the horse all over
22 Flexing for calm
24 Putting horse whispering to use
24 The hidden secrets of horse whispering

WHAT IS HORSE WHISPERING?

Throughout history there have been people famed for their exceptional abilities with horses. The tale of how the young Alexander the Great tamed the reputedly wild horse Bucephalus, by understanding that the horse was afraid of its own shadow, is an early example. In more recent centuries, people with incredible horsemanship skills have been referred to as 'horse whisperers'. In the nineteenth century, an American farmer called Rarey thrilled audiences on both sides of the Atlantic with his horse-taming skills; in the twentieth century, people like Tom Dorrance and Monty Roberts raised much interest in how we interact with our horses.

Horse whispering is often thought of as working magic or spells with horses, but horse whispering is a broad term that describes subtle ways of influencing and communicating with horses. The word 'whispering' is used because the signals between the horse and human can be so subtle and quiet as to be like a whisper, so it appears that the human has whispered something and the horse, having understood, changes its behaviour.

By 'talking' the horse's own language and understanding the horse's nature, we can learn to develop ways to interact more effectively with these wonderful creatures and achieve fantastic results for ourselves and our horses. The methods and results of horse whispering sometimes appear so amazing that it is easy to see why people in the past thought horse whisperers were more like magicians, rather than fine horsemen.

Of course, some horse whisperers work with wild or very difficult problem horses, but it is important to realise that they have been practising the art of horse whispering for many years. Difficult or real 'problem horses' are best left to professional experts to sort out.

In this book we will be looking at various horse-whispering techniques and principles that can help you to develop better bonds with horses, hopefully with some 'magical' results. As a bonus, you may find some difficulties with horses gradually disappear on their own as you become more practised and skilful at horse whispering.

TIMID

TIMID This posture is not very helpful with horses. It tends to make nervous horses feel even more nervous and can make many other horses walk all over you! This says, 'I'm nervous, small and insignificant – stand on me, push me about, knock me over or bite me if you want.'

INVISIBLE Incredible inner stillness, your eyes, body and movements become invisible, like you're no longer there any more. Sometimes horses can get so emotionally fraught that they need you to be passive to the point that you're no longer a visible presence. Come back to being visible again when their emotions have settled, and they'll be delighted to see you.

ACCIDENTALLY INVISIBLE The other type of 'invisible' is where you appear totally insignificant and get into the wrong place at the wrong time, with the wrong horse, and the horse doesn't see you – and you get hurt. Horse whisperers very rarely do 'Accidentally Invisible'!

INVISIBLE

ACCIDENTALLY INVISIBLE

OVERALL VOLUME Within each of the above postures there can be many gradual increases and decreases in 'volume', e.g. Positive posture could start so softly that it is almost a Passive posture; with a gradual increase in volume you make yourself bigger, until it turns into a Dominant posture. It means, as a horse whisperer, that you have many levels of expression with which to talk to horses. This is useful because every horse is different, and while some horses may need louder body language, many other horses require your body language to be very, very quiet for them to not be too skittish or frightened.

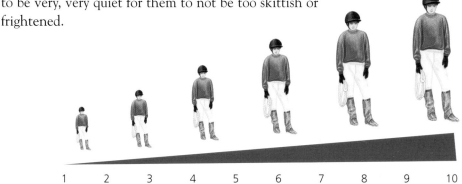

1   2   3   4   5   6   7   8   9   10

11

Hand, Voice and Breathing Signals

Signals with your hands

Generally speaking, the less we use our hands around horses, the better. There are, however, a few subtleties that can be useful in getting our message across.

FINGERS WIDE OPEN, arms hanging, palms facing the horse – useful in a round pen to ask horses to move on more: the hands imitate predator's claws.

FISTS CLOSED TIGHT – makes us appear more firm and have a stronger stance.

HAND(S) HELD UP IN FRONT OF YOU, between you and the horse with palms facing the horse – this is a blocking signal to help stop the horse from coming closer or taking over your space.

USING THE BACK OF THE HAND to stroke the horse – some sensitive horses prefer this since the back of the hand is less like a claw.

Use of the voice

Most horse communication, and therefore most of the horse whisperer's, is done using body language. It is sometimes useful, however, to use sounds to help you with horses, but these are best used sparingly. As we humans are so used to relying on words to talk to each other, it is easy to start forgetting about your body language with the horse if you talk too much!

Sounds like 'aaaaaah!', that are low in pitch and drop down as they go on, are helpful in bringing the horse's energy level down or to relax him.

Whistling with a downwards slide in pitch is also useful for bringing the horse to relaxation. Whistling also puts you at your ease as well as letting the horse know you are not another horse, as horses can't whistle.

Humming quietly has a relaxing effect on horses. Quite a number of horses 'hum' to themselves as they walk along in a relaxed way when out hacking.

Using your breath

Horses and humans have very similar breathing patterns, and because of this, the way you are breathing tells the horse something about how you are feeling in a way that he understands.

Keeping a check on your breathing is a very useful method of staying in control of a situation, and sighing loudly a few times is a handy way to take a horse's energy level down.

GETTING HORSES TO FOLLOW YOU – METHOD 1

You will need

For this method you will need a round pen, or any safe space such as a small paddock or riding arena, in which you can let the horse loose.

You will also need a rope, a lunge line, or something similar, in your hand that you can swing towards the horse to motivate him, if necessary.

IMPORTANT NOTE – This method is not suitable for horses with lameness, stiffness, or serious mental problems, or for horses under three years old.

Mental attitude

It is important that you carry out this method in a calm, unemotional way, without shouting or getting angry, impatient or frustrated. You do not want to upset the horse. The horse will be trying his best to figure out what is expected of him in this situation and he may not understand you immediately. Be kind and persistent, and be pleased with very small results to begin with.

Getting started

Stand in the middle of the pen and stroke the horse to let him know you are a friend and that being with you is pleasant.

Now look directly at the horse with your eyes and body. Adopt the positive or dominant posture, starting with your body fairly quiet and increase the volume of your posture until he moves away. If you need help sending the horse away from you, stay out of kicking range and start swinging the rope towards the horse behind the saddle area.

NOTE: Some horses are sensitive, so your body language may only need to be very quiet for them to go away from you; some horses are more laid-back and your body language will have to be louder.

Staying out of the way
Make sure you don't stand in front of the horse or 'get in his way', otherwise he will slow down, stop or change direction.

Once the horse is moving, stand in the centre of the pen as much as possible.

The horse may choose to trot or canter. If he is calm enough you may ask him to move on a little, although with some sensitive horses this method can even work in walk.

Your body language
Follow his eye with your eyes, your body facing his body, and only swing the rope if he

tries to slow down, stop without you asking, or if he tries to change direction without your permission.

The horse's body language
Read the horse's body language as he goes round the pen.

- If his head and ears are away from you, ask him to keep moving.

- If he turns his ears or head towards you, comes in closer on the circle or drops his head and licks his lips, drop your eyes down and change your body into a soft, passive posture. Back away from him a step or two to and invite him to stop if he is ready. (If he carries on at the same speed regardless of your invitation, bring your body back up to 'positive' again and ask him to keep going for a while longer.)

Creating the connection

If he stops when you lower your eyes and body: Good.

If he moves even one step towards you or even just stands looking at you: Great.

Quietly walk over to his shoulder (with your body and eyes still softly passive) and stand and stroke him for a minute or two.

The horse following you

Now is his chance to choose to follow you. Casually walk away from the horse's shoulder in an arc, feeling for an invisible connection between you and him. Don't walk directly in front of him at this stage as he is less likely to choose to follow; instead, walk away from his shoulder at an angle (see drawings below).

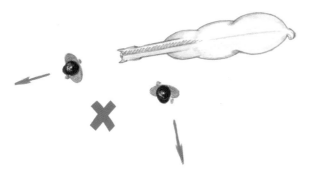

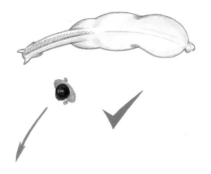

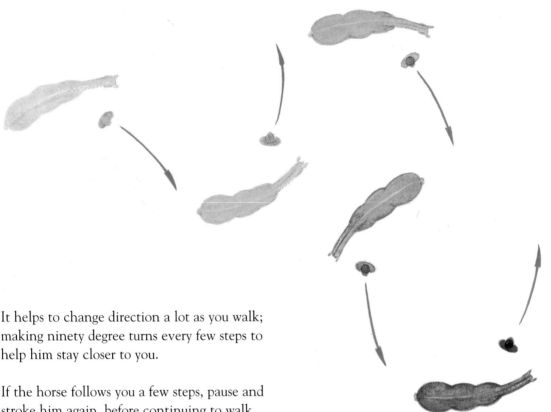

It helps to change direction a lot as you walk; making ninety degree turns every few steps to help him stay closer to you.

If the horse follows you a few steps, pause and stroke him again, before continuing to walk. If the horse follows for a while then chooses to leave, you can always send him off around the pen again a couple of times to let him think about the wisdom of his decision not to follow you, then give him another chance to stop.

Waiting for the connection

If the horse doesn't follow you at all and you've given him a little time to think about it, quietly send him off around the pen again, this time in the other direction. Again watch for signs from the horse that he is ready for another chance to follow you, and if so, drop your positive posture and allow him to stop again for you to stroke him.

Explanation This method works by using the horse's natural desire for company. By making the horse move away from you, and then allowing him to be with you, you establish a desire in the horse for the safe and comfortable connection of being close to you.

If you introduce a new horse to a herd, the herd horses will usually make it stay on the outside of the herd until it gives the same signs as you are looking for in the pen, then they will let it join the safety of the herd.

GETTING HORSES TO FOLLOW YOU – METHOD 2

Equipment
The handy thing about this method is that it doesn't need a round pen or enclosed area to begin; it requires only a halter and rope (preferably about 12ft/3.6m long) and a stick (about 3ft/1m or 4ft/1.2m long).

Attitude
As with method 1, it is important to maintain a calm, kind attitude and to give the horse time to figure out what you want.

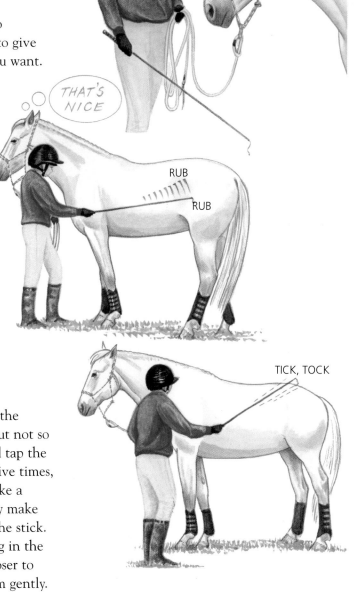

THAT'S NICE

RUB

RUB

TICK, TOCK

Getting started
Once again, begin by stroking the horse on both sides of his body and head. You also need to stroke the horse on his hindquarters with the stick until he is not afraid of it.

Now stand slightly to one side of the horse, have the rope a little slack, but not so slack that he can walk forwards, and tap the air gently in a slow rhythm four or five times, near his hindquarters (tap-tap-tap like a ticking grandfather clock). This may make him move his hind end away from the stick. If he doesn't move, continue tapping in the same rhythm and move the stick closer to him so that it is actually tapping him gently.

Response

As soon as the horse moves the slightest bit away from the stick, stop tapping with the stick and stroke him with it instead. If you have the rope at the right length you will notice that when he moves his hind end away from the stick, his head comes around closer to you. Now stroke his forehead softly between his eyes.

Repeat the process until his head comes closer to you each time.

Creating the connection

Next, as his head comes around towards you, take a step or two away from him while he is still moving, making sure the rope stays slack. As you move away, feel the connection between you, and he should step towards you with his head.

Build on this until you can walk around with the rope totally slack and he follows you as you turn this way and that. Practise this as though the rope didn't exist and then, in a safe place, start with the rope and then try with the rope unclipped.

Choices

There will be times when a horse follows you brilliantly and other times when the same horse may not bother much at all. It is important to remember that horses are sentient beings with minds of their own, therefore they are free to make their own choices. It is easier and far less frustrating for us if we remember this fact and expect that they will not always make choices that totally suit us!

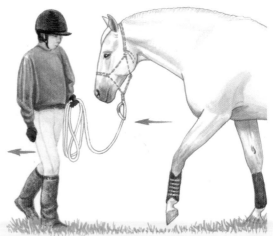

LEADERSHIP, BODY SPACE AND BOUNDARIES

Horses are very aware of their personal body space and what it means. A herd leader will step into a subordinate's body space and will even give the underling a push so that it has to move itself out of the way. Horses do this to us too if we're not aware of it.

YOUR PERSONAL SPACE Decide for yourself what constitutes a comfortable area of personal space around you, and use your body language to make horses stick to this boundary of yours by not allowing them to come any closer. You may need to keep some horses further from you than others. Horses that barge, are pushy or bite, for example, are best kept further from you than more polite individuals.

Decide never to let horses push into your space or make you step backward. While you may not notice when you are stepping backwards out of a horse's way, you can be sure the horse does. This is the kind of thing the horse whisperer notices, as otherwise he/she would be telling the horse that it is the leader.

If the lead horse is the one that makes the other horse move its feet or its whole self out of the way, try getting your horse to step back away from you with your body language. Make yourself big and take up a bit of the space that the horse has.

> **IMPORTANT**
>
> **Remember to stroke the horse before and after doing this.**
>
> **LEADERS ALWAYS SHOW THEY CARE**

TAMING THE WILD SIDE

Horses can be lively and wild creatures. What the horse whisperer sometimes does is allow the horse to express his excess energy – but at a safe distance.

If you have a horse with too much energy, in a safe enclosure, let him loose to 'run it off' and be the wild beautiful creature that he is. What you do is stay out of the way by standing quietly in the middle of the area, so that in one way you are still a part of what is happening, but in another way you are waiting for the horse to be ready to be with you.

He can be as wild and expressive as he likes, provided he does it at a safe distance from you.

Sometimes it is too difficult for the horse and for the human to hold or contain 'wild' horse energy, so the best thing to do is let him run around the edge of an enclosure, while you stand in the middle.

As the horse whisperer, you ask yourself (and answer honestly) if the horse has finished running off his wild side, then you go over to him again and get on with whatever you were going to do together in a far more civilised fashion. The fact that you were there in the middle while he expressed himself makes him think that, in part, you tamed his wild side (whereas, in fact, all you did was stood and waited for him to be ready for you).

RUNNING WITH HORSES

To be a horse whisperer requires you to know horses inside-out. The best way to do that is not just to see them in the stable or on the yard; you need to go out and get amongst them when they are at liberty together in the herd.

Make a point of watching horses in the pasture and studying what they do together. If the herd is safe enough, go in amongst them, be with them for a while, watch what they do and how they interact, then you can do the same. If they run or canter round the field, run with them. It is a fantastic feeling to run with a herd of horses, and so often

they love you to join in too.

As well as running with them, have a doze with them when they have a doze. Get into some mutual grooming too!

Be very careful to be safe at all times when you are around loose horses – they certainly can play rough sometimes.

THE MAGIC TOUCH – STROKING THE HORSE ALL OVER

From time to time we all give horses a little stroke or a pat, but touching every part of the horse's body can have a transforming and calming effect on the horse.

When – Obviously if a horse is thrashing around it is not an ideal time to try this. If the horse is a little agitated, it may be safe to try. Have the horse on a halter and longish lead rope so that you have some control and connection to start with.

How – Have your body in a passive posture. Use your hand (or a stick, if you need to be a safer distance away from the horse) in slow, smooth strokes with a regular rhythm so that it is as pleasurable as possible. (Think how you would like to be stroked yourself.) Because the horse's brain is split into two almost completely separate halves, left and right, it is important to stroke both sides of the horse equally, left and right.

Start with the horse's mane and crest, the sides of the neck and shoulders. Move down his spine towards his hindquarters, then come back to the neck, this time also doing the underside of his neck down to between the front legs.

Now go up to the area between his eyes and his poll. See if you can gently rub his ears and muzzle. Some horses are touchy about the ears, which may mean they fuss about the bridle, whilst others even like you scratching inside their ears, and go into a trance.

Some horses are touchy about the muzzle, which may mean they are uncomfortable about bridles and bits or may be inclined to rear. Gently put your fingers in the side of the horse's mouth and touch the tongue. Also try putting a finger up between the front top teeth and the top lip, gently rubbing the gum – this can also send some horses into a trance of pleasure.

Now go back to the neck and, in one movement, without taking a hand off, go from the shoulder, along the spine, down the hindquarters and down the back leg all the way to the hock. (Horses are long animals, so this is a good way of reminding the horse that his back legs belong to him.)

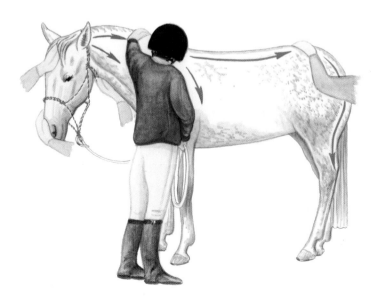

THE MAGIC TOUCH (CONT.)

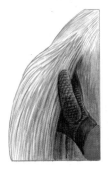

Remember to stroke the horse's tail; horses have a lot of feeling in the tail as it is part of the lower spine. The stiffness or relaxation of the tail can tell you how safe and relaxed the horse is feeling. If he lets you stroke the soft underside near the top of his tail, he trusts you and feels relaxed; if he clamps his tail down, he is being defensive.

Although we pick horses' feet up to shoe them and clean them, we can also pick up their feet as a means of exploring the relationship between us and them. The horse's feet are his natural means of escape and survival, so if he gives you his feet it is a very trusting thing.

Many horses pick up their feet but hold tension in the leg. As part of the magic touch of horse whispering, pick up a horse's front foot with one hand, then use the other hand to stroke his shoulder or upper leg until you feel him soften inside the leg you are holding. Do the same with the hind feet, stroking his croup with your spare hand until he softens and trusts you more.

FLEXING FOR CALM

If the horse is not too wild and lively, but is still a little distracted and tense, you can use this method to calm him. For safety's sake it may be best to have him in a halter.

To begin Stand in a passive position near the horse's shoulder, face slightly towards

him, and give him a gentle stroking.

Now place the hand nearest his head softly on his nose about where the halter goes. Apply very gentle pressure with your fingertips to the side of his nose you can't see, inviting him to turn his head around towards you.

If he brings his head towards you, soften your finger pressure, relax your body and breathe out with a sigh to let him know this is good. Let him have his head turned to you for five seconds or so and then quietly let go. Walk around the other side of the horse and repeat the other way. It is important to do both sides of the horse equally.

If he tosses his head around, stay quiet and softly follow his head with your hand still in the same place on his head, being calmly persistent until he turns his head to you.

If he starts moving his feet about, stay quiet and still follow with your hand in the same place on his head until he settles and turns his head to follow you.

Did you notice if the horse is stiffer on one side? This tells you a lot about how he might be to ride – how he will be more responsive to the bit on one side of his mouth and how he may be stiffer in his hind leg on that side too.

Some people do this exercise using a carrot or a titbit to get the horse to flex his head around: that does not really serve the same purpose as the method described above, as a titbit doesn't teach the horse to yield to you when he feels light pressure.

Asking for backward steps After you have flexed the horse's head each way, you may find asking for a few backwards steps helps to bring him even more 'under your wing'. It is important, as with all the things you do around horses, that you are very quiet and calm, and that you keep the horse calm too.

Getting started Stand in front of the horse and stroke his head. Now place your hand lightly on his nose where the halter goes and apply very gentle pressure, asking him to take a step backward. If he doesn't understand, you can assist by using your other hand to apply light pressure to the front of his chest at the same time.

As soon as he steps back, release him from the pressure of your hands and stroke him again. This is how he will learn to be light and responsive to you, as well as becoming more calm and gentle.

PUTTING HORSE WHISPERING TO USE

Experimenting with some of the techniques of horse whispering can be great fun in itself – and there is almost nothing more satisfying than enjoying the special connection you can achieve with horses – but there are further benefits to horse whispering that help in other situations.

General handling Horses trust you more, become easier to catch, lead, shoe, groom, load, etc.; you don't need to get angry, frightened or shout anymore, and horses feel happier because they know you speak 'horse'.

Riding Once you have a connection on the ground, the horse and you naturally have a closer connection when you are in the saddle. If the horse wants to be with you on the ground, he'll also want to be with you on his back. You are both speaking more of the same language and understanding each other more, so the horse and you will both be willing and able to go that extra mile together for each other, as partners, friends and as a team when you are schooling or competing.

THE HIDDEN SECRETS OF HORSE WHISPERING

In this book we have looked at some of the practical methods of horse whispering, but maybe there is more to it than that? Well, there certainly can be, and by practising horse whispering and being kind, loving and understanding to horses at all times, maybe you too will find the hidden secrets of horse whispering for yourself.